Unleashing the L.E.A.D. in Leadership

Lisa Nanches Jackson

Elshamar Desktop Publishing

Unleashing the L.E.A.D. in Leadership
Copyright © 2019 Lisa Nanches Jackson

Cover Image: SPJ Graphic Designs, Inc.

ISBN 13: 978-0-97480066-0

This book is dedicated to my family (husband Carl, daughter Tierra, and mother Golethia). The tremendous love, support, and the confidence that you have shown me has been the wind beneath my wings. You consistently believe that I can do anything and now I do too! I would also like to thank my spiritual parents/pastors Archbishop Alfred A. Owens, Jr. and Co-Pastor Susie C. Owens who gave me an opportunity to lead. I would also like to thank Dr. Wanda Frazier-Parker for her love, encouragement and the impact she has had in my life.

This is the second of a three-part series. This series will be a necessary resource to add to every great leader's library.

1. **Activating** the L. E. A. D. in Leadership

2. **Igniting** the L. E. A. D. in Leadership

3. **Unleashing** the L. E. A. D. in Leadership

Preface

According to the Oxford dictionary, the word unleash means to let loose, release, free, set free. The term fire is a passionate emotion. There comes a time in a leader's life that he/she must put into practice that has been learned. Great leaders have the right and responsibility to release what they have learned so that those they lead are better. One key characteristics of a great leader is being resourceful. This author often said that I might not know everything, but I will find the answer. This volume has been penned to serve as a resource to help the leader, find an answer.

GREAT leaders recognize that they are free to lead in unconventional ways that impact and empower their followers to take a risk in their quest to be the best that they can be. It is a tool that will help with maximizing the readers effectiveness in a multigenerational workplace.

Table of Contents

FOREWORD

Countless books, publications, and periodicals address the ongoing mission to become better leaders, thereby continuing the rhythm of successful leadership. **Great** leaders are open to continued learning and encourage others to become their best in more than one sphere of influence through study, research, and rehearsing what other **great** leaders have done. With relentless conviction from personal, governmental, and Christian leadership experience, Lisa Nanches Jackson heralds that all leaders must maintain integrity and character as we lead others. Her approach to leadership is that we bring our authentic self to the table and establish trust with those we are leading. ***This 3-part L.E.A.D. Series*** provides any leader with a comprehensive approach to take their leadership from good to **great**. Volume 1, ***Activating the L.E.A.D. in Leadership*** admonishes leaders to acknowledge blind spots, weaknesses, and challenges that impede effective leadership in contemporary times. Volume 2, ***IGNITING the L.E.A.D. in Leadership*** provides the reader with insight on how to recognize the hidden potential in those they lead, so that they encourage and enhance the possibility of achievement in the follower. This is a powerful tool and if used properly can propel the follower beyond a level of achievement they never expected. Volume 3, ***UNLEASHING the L.E.A.D. in Leadership***, is a resource guide that every leader needs to have in their arsenal. It is full of strategic plans, best practices, tools, and techniques that will enable the leader to continually grow in his/her quest to go from good to **great**.

Secure leaders are passionate about developing leaders around them for success and continued growth in the organization. The practical applications at the end of each segment allow the "learning-leader" to be accountable. Accountability is as much practical as it is marketable in the 21st century. Leaders who make the commitment to lead by example and not through the positional power are in high demand, especially among millennials. Consequently, rethinking how we lead in the 21st century can be challenging but is necessary when addressing the needs of ever-changing, ever-learning demographic.

This L.E.A.D. Series will motivate leaders to recalibrate and re-brand your leadership approach and style.

I sincerely recommend This L.E.A.D. Series. It will prove to be a how-to tool. It's creative, loaded with multi-generational leadership applications yet profound in clarity and upward movement. If you are new in your leadership career, this is an excellent model to jump-start your journey. If you are an experienced leader, this tool will galvanize your authentic leadership style and approach.

Let's push the restart button on leadership to influence, impact, and add value to those who follow us! Continue as a learning leader, encourage others to be better than yourself (which is authentic leadership), and remain committed to the cause for which you are most passionate.

Leading on Purpose,
Dr. Wanda Frazier-Parker
Certified Coach, Speaker, Teacher & Trainer
Empowered for Living

Unleashing the **L. E. A. D.** in Leadership

Learner
Encourager
Authentic
Determined

Once we Activate the L.E.A.D. in Leadership the next step is to Ignite it and finally we must Unleash it! This book will provide the reader with the tools to ignite the flame of potential in those they lead, so that it burns brightly and propels them to their next level of greatness.

There is a great debate about whether leaders are born or made, but I submit to you, there is no debate that if we are going to be effective, we must be intentional about leading. The author shares what she has gleaned, discovered and imparted through her 26 years of leadership.

Great leaders are life-long **learners**. They are wise enough to know that relevant, impactful leadership is a journey and not a destination. It is essential that the leader periodically performs a Self-assessment or Value Audit. Take an inventory of your unique talents and strengths. Also know your weaknesses, hopes, worries, fears, and goals. Becoming familiar with these areas will give guidance to the direction you should take when considering growth strategies.

Great leaders are **encouragers**. They inspire with courage and confidence. They are purposeful in identifying and developing the seed of greatness that lies in those they lead. When we look at the word 'encouragement', we see included in the word another word, courage. Encouragement can be like fuel to a person that is running on empty. **Great** leaders impart courage to those they lead. They do so by taking the time to look beyond the surface.

Great leaders are **authentic**. They are sincere and serious about developing others. They treat people the way they want to be treated. They aren't wrapped up in their leadership positional power, they don't look down on others or pretend to be interested in their followers, and they are genuine. An authentic leader can be a lifeline to a follower. When leaders are authentic, it lets those we lead know we are not perfect. We should continue to strive for perfection. Authentic leaders let those following them know it is okay to ask/receive help.

Great leaders are **determined**. They are purposeful and unwavering in their commitment and cause to influence, direct, and guide others. Leaders embrace a can-do attitude. They refuse to quit and defy the odds against them.

As stated in volumes one and two of this series, the commitment to continue to learn, encouragement and authenticity to those you lead leaving people better off than when you encountered them is value added.

Whether you are a leader, supervisor, manager, or a CEO this Resource Guide filled with the 'Best Practices' will enhance your ability to be the best you can be. Unleashing the LEAD in Leadership will provide you with helpful answers and information on "How To . . .".

"The unsuccessful person is burdened by learning and prefers to walk down familiar paths. Their distaste for learning stunts their growth and limits their influence."

- John C. Maxwell

Chapter One

Handling Non-compliance by Employees

In the face a challenge,
be confident and courageous.

- Lisa Nanches Jackson

Non-compliance is the failure of an employee to act in accordance with the workplace policies and rules, or the inability to meet specified criterions. When employees are non-compliant, it can interfere with the mission of the organization being fulfilled, it can affect other employees' morale, and failure to effectively deal with noncompliant employees can diminish one's authority as the supervisor or manager.

An important factor to note is that everyone in the workplace is there to do a job. It is crucial for this factor to remain the focus and employees are held accountable. Accountability means that everyone is responsible for their own actions. **Great** leaders use accountable to empower their employees. For you see, it is a matter of perspective. Responsibility can be seen in a positive and negative light. It's the leader's responsibility to present it in the most positive light. One tactic for the supervisor\leader is to show the employee how the added responsibility helps them. One of the points I often make to people is once you have a skill or learn something it belongs to you. Therefore, you can choose to use it in your present position and future position. With additional skills and responsibility comes more opportunity. This is a positive light.

I found throughout my career that most people desire to feel needed; Quite frankly when someone is responsible for something it helps them feel needed. However, it is essential that people are properly equipped to handle the responsibility. When they are properly equipped, they are set-up to succeed. Sadly, many people have been given more responsibility without being properly equipped and ultimately fail. The good news is that you can change this paradigm and change the experience of a non-compliant employee. Below, you will find what I like to call the "Triple E" approach to effectively handling non-compliant employees.

Encourage – Give the employee mental support and hope that they have what it takes to do the job and that they CAN achieve the status of a productive employee.

Equip – Provide the employee with the training and mentoring they need to understand and accomplish their work.

Prepare them mentally that it will require them to give 100% but let them know they have the needed tools and the know how to be successful in doing their jobs.

Empower – Confronting the deficiency can cause an employee to be stronger in their skill level and more confident in completing his/her work.

Handling non-compliant employees can be both challenging and rewarding. There are many challenges that leaders/supervisors face. However, when you have invested in yourself and your ability to lead you will be up for the challenge. The rewards of seeing the success of an employee that has taken on a

new and positive attitude are priceless!

ARE YOU READY?

_____

_____

_____

_____

_____

_____

_____

_____

_____

_____

_____

_____

ARE YOU READY?

_____

_____

_____

_____

_____

_____

_____

_____

_____

_____

_____

Chapter Two

Effective Motivation Tools

It is human nature to want to correct rather than compliment. Do not give into your nature.

- Lisa Nanches Jackson

Let's face it; the environment and fiscal climate of the workforce have drastically changed. This change has caused GREAT leaders to find alternative cost-effective ways to motivate their staff. It has been my experience that effectively motivating staff can increase productivity and enhance the work environment. Many people spend a large part of their day working. Depending upon the nature of work it can be stressful and unrewarding. It becomes the role of a **GREAT** leader to come alongside the employee or follower to help motivate the person. There is a school of thought that motivation should come from within and that is correct. However, life has a way of challenging one's ability to muster up the motivation. There are times when a leader can provide a "jump start" of motivation and it will give the employee/team member the charge they need to keep it going.

My experience has found that "praise or verbal recognition," can be effective motivation tools. Recently the phrase, "see something – say something," has been coined. This phrase can be applied in the workforce or in any setting one leads. According to a published study "The Role of Positivity and

Connectivity in the Performance of Business Teams: A Nonlinear Dynamics Model," conducted by academic Emily Heaphy and consultant Marcial Losada[i]., it takes five compliments to make up for one criticism. The full study can be found at doi.org. This study shows the significance positive verbal recognition can have on an employee's performance. The challenge for the leader is to be intentional about looking for something good to say about the employee's performance or the value the employee brings to the workplace. It can sometimes be a challenge because it's easier to see what is not

right or how something could be better.
However, it takes intentionality to mention
the positive. It is human nature to want to
correct rather than compliment. Do not give
into your nature! I have found that if you look
hard enough there is something
complimentary you can say about your
employee(s). Try beginning every
conversation with something positive, it will
make the constructive criticism easier to
receive.

A Peer Recognition Program can be an
effective motivational tool. The program
involves peers in recognizing the

achievements of peers. This is particularly effective in larger office settings, because the supervisor/manager may not have the opportunity to see all the day-in-day-out staff achievements. Implementing this tool is cost-effective. The idea is for the staff to submit an email or note to the supervisor monthly, which nominates a co-worker for recognition based upon something done. There are times when an employee might submit his/her own name, if the accomplishment is valid, it should not be ignored. The supervisor then recognizes the person, with the most nominations during the staff meeting. It is suggested that an employee recognition item be added to the monthly agenda. This lets the employees know that this is important. The supervisor can issue a certificate of appreciation or in some instances a day-off award.

The" Super Star Award," can also be a motivation tool. The idea for this tool is for the supervisor to purchase or create gold stars, it should be noted that the star should be large enough to post, perhaps a 6 x 6 size. When a staff member does something that is worth recognizing he/she is given a star. The star is posted somewhere in the employee's area for them and all to see. You can put what they did on the star or just give them the star. There can be a quarterly recognition of the staff member who has accumulated the most stars. That person could receive a free lunch or a gift card or movie ticket or something that you deem appropriate. This is a small investment in the lives of those you lead. A **GREAT** leader will find a way to invest in the success of those they lead.

ARE YOU READY?

_____

_____

_____

_____

_____

_____

_____

_____

_____

_____

_____

_____

ARE YOU READY?

_____

_____

_____

_____

_____

_____

_____

_____

_____

_____

_____

ARE YOU READY?

_____

_____

_____

_____

_____

_____

_____

_____

_____

_____

Chapter Three

Influencing Staff Who Have "Retired in Place"

A courageous conversation that is strategic, provides clear parameters for change and is goal oriented.

- Lisa Nanches Jackson

In my 34 years of public service, I have encountered people that have become discontent with their jobs, tired of working or lost motivation to be the best they could be. The people became content with collecting a paycheck without putting in the work to receive it. Due to their lack of productivity, these people were labeled as "retired in place." Meaning, their mentality was retirement and their behavior was retired, but they were still actually coming to work, not working and collecting a paycheck. Unfortunately, for both the organization and the employee, this type of behavior has become acceptable in the name of keeping the peace. **Great** leaders realize that it helps the employee and the organization to challenge the status quo. With the right influence, employees that are unmotivated and under-motivated can change and return to an acceptable level of productivity. A **Great** leader possess the capacity to influence the character, development, or behavior of an employee or team member.

The key to returning unmotivated and under-motivated employees to an acceptable level of productivity is to be willing to have courageous conversations. The question then becomes what a courageous conversation is. It is a conversation that is strategic, provides clear parameters for change and is goal oriented. It is a conversation that may be uncomfortable for the leader and the follower. A courageous conversation is a conversation that is respectful, yet direct. It is a conversation that confronts but is not necessarily confrontational. A courageous conversation is one that might initially seem stern, but ultimately (if handled correctly) becomes empowering.

Best Practices to follow addressing an employee who has "retired in place":

1) Own the agency management's role in permitting the behavior. Oftentimes, the behavior has been allowed to continue for years.

2) Set-up a meeting with the employee.

3) Come up with a plan to assist the employee in returning to acceptable performance. This can often begin with reviewing the employee's Work Plan and assessing the needed areas of improvement. The next step is to ask yourself some relevant questions and document your answers. Question one is

what needs to happen regarding the

employee. Question two is how you plan

to initiate the change. Question three is

how you can ensure that the change will be

sustainable. Question four is how you will

measure success. The fifth and final

question is what you will do if the

employee refuses to change. These are real

and relevant questions that must be

addressed in the process of coming up with

a plan to return an employee to acceptable

performance. Keep in mind the plan

should follow the SMART model. The

goals should be **S**pecific, **M**easurable,

Actionable, Relevant, and Time-bound.

Using this tool will add structure to your

goals. '*Specific*' challenges you to clearly

define how long the change should take

and how you plan to measure success.

'*Measurable*' challenges you to have a

concrete way to tell if progress is being

made. '*Actionable*' challenges you to come

up with an action plan. Relevant

challenges you to keep the main thing the

main thing, which is the employee

returning to an acceptable level of

performance. Finally, '*Time-bound*'

challenges you to designate a reasonable

amount of time to see improvement. The goal of this process is to help the employee succeed, so he/she should be given a fair amount of time. If possible, allow a minimum of three-months.

ARE YOU READY?

_____

_____

_____

_____

_____

_____

_____

_____

_____

_____

_____

ARE YOU READY?

ARE YOU READY?

_____

_____

_____

_____

_____

_____

_____

_____

_____

_____

_____

Chapter Four

Accountability is Key

Until a leader equips the follower with the proper tools to be successful, the leader is held accountable for the lack of success.

- Lisa Nanches Jackson

Great leaders are accountable and hold others accountable too. According to the Oxford Dictionary accountability is defined as, "The fact or condition of being accountable; responsibility." In other words, one is answerable for their actions and decisions. There is a duty to own one's actions and areas of influence.

Accountability is key because it causes one to take ownership. If an assignment has a due date then that date should be met, otherwise there must be consequences for the failure to meet the deadline.

The consequences can vary depending upon the urgency or importance of the assignment. **GREAT** leaders provide their followers with the needed to do their job. Those tools could be informal or formal training. It is only after someone has been given the tools to be successful that they can be held accountable for the success in completing the task. Until a leader equips the follower or the employee with the proper tools to be successful, the leader is held accountable for the lack of success.

Effective communication is essential for accountability. The expectations must be shared and understood if one is going to be held accountable. It is not reasonable to hold people accountable for "what they should have known." The reality is that the workplace is multi-generational. This means that there are: Centennials, Millennials, Generation X, Baby Boomers, and Traditionalists, people born in different generations coming together to get the job done. With this level of diversity, there may be people who are in the Centennial and Millennial generations who are entering the workforce and have no idea about historical protocol; They may have no idea about the policies and procedures or the workforce and they may not fully comprehend the manual, because they fail to see the importance. This population needs to be met with understanding and the willingness to articulate those things that need to be done as instructed while extending the openness to consider those things that can be done differently to achieve the same goal. Conversely, there are Baby Boomers and Traditionalists that may have been working in the office for a long time and they may be reluctant to change. This population, too, needs to be met with understanding and the leader should exhibit a willingness to articulate the changes with patience. Once the proper training has occurred, the employee or follower can be held accountable for performance. When communicating, it is important to remember tone matters, so always be respectful acknowledging the value of the employee or follower.

I conclude this section with three keys of accountability to consider:

1) *Accountability* must be applicable to all, including the leader,

2) *Clear Communication* regarding expectations is necessary and

3) *Proper training* is essential. It is always important to exercise the Golden Rule, which is to treat others like you want to be treated.

ARE YOU READY?

_____

_____

_____

_____

_____

_____

_____

_____

_____

_____

_____

ARE YOU READY?

_____

_____

_____

_____

_____

_____

_____

_____

_____

_____

Chapter Five

Why Should People Vote for You? Core Leadership Skills

It is not the desire of others that makes one a leader. It takes intentionality on behalf of the potential leader to aid him/her in their leadership quest.

- Lisa Nanches Jackson

Today, it is crucial that children are trained and prepared for a positive path. **GREAT** leaders equip the next generation because they realize the importance. Children are so advanced. They are exposed to tools and technology at a very young age. This exposure not only challenges them, but it also challenges those they encounter. My goddaughter is 6-years old. She was recently tested as a part of the school's acceptance policy. I was astonished to learn that the entire test was administered on a computer. Her parents were not allowed to be in the room while she was being tested. I am proud to say that she was accepted! This scenario presents a very real portrait of the children of today. There is a need to cultivate and channel this level of intelligence in ways that we are molding the leaders of tomorrow.

One of the ways young people can be trained or cultivated into leaders is through the avenue of a Student Council. According to the Oxford Dictionary, a Student Council is a group of students elected by their peers to address issues of concern and organize student events and activities. My 11-year-old niece recently came to me and told me she wanted to be the president of her six-grade class. This was very exciting for the family. We got busy pooling our efforts to prep her and to ensure that she was prepared to run her campaign. The next day I realized that we were so excited with the possibility of her becoming president that I never asked her a critical question. The question was, "why should people vote for you?" When I asked the question, it was met with silence it was at that point I realized that we would be doing her a disservice if we did all the prep work and pushed her into a presidency for which she was not equipped. The next day I began assessing her leadership skills and training her on the fundamentals of being a leader. Following the assessment and training, she was able to give me a good answer to my initial question. She said, she felt that she could share the students concerns and make a positive difference. As of the writing of this book the votes are still pending, but I can say that she is now ready to lead.

When a student exhibits some of the core leadership skills listed below, they are good candidates to lead.

- **Courage** – this is simply standing up for what one believes. However, it requires that one knows what he or she believes.

- **Interpersonal Skills** – is the ability to clear communication and the willingness to work with others.

- **Decision Making** – is the ability to make good decisions. Further, it is the process of deciding something important, especially in a group of people or in an organization.
  - It is Systemic or a Process.
  - What's the worst thing that could happen from the decision?
  - How would you deal with it?
  - What's the best thing that could happen from the decision?
  - Be willing to own your decisions.

- A practical system that includes some level of critical thinking is essential.

Critical Thinking means:
  - Stepping back from your bias
  - Examining data from different angles
  - Checking the accuracy of information

- Checking the logic of the argument
- Looking for possible flaws in the argument
- Understanding why other people see it differently
- Checking statistics and other empirical data
- Checking unacknowledged self-truths
- Reaching informed conclusions

- **Conflict Management** – this is the ability to effectively manage conflict or areas of disagreement with others or a group of others. It involves collaboration and compromise to facilitate a win-win situation.

- **Influence** – this is the power to fairly and effectively inspire or impact a person or group of people.

- **Problem-Solving Skills** – Someone who makes themselves an answer. They embrace and understand the concept of making problems work for them. Essentially, there are 3 Ways Problems Can Work for Us:

- Problems can introduce us to ourselves.
- Problems can introduce us to others.
- Problems can introduce us to opportunities.

The student has the potential to be a great leader. It is important that the student is encouraged, not pushed, but encouraged to pursue some form of leadership. The student must first be encouraged to lead him/herself. This is successfully done when they make good decisions, when they are obedient, and when they are willing to look beyond themselves and consider the needs of others.

There are some serious questions that should be considered and contemplated by those who are considering running for a leadership position.

1. Why do you want to be in the position?

2. How do you believe that you can contribute to the betterment of the people?

3. What do you plan to do to make a positive difference?

4. Why should people vote for you?

These questions should be answered before embarking upon a leadership position. It is not the desire of others that makes one a good or **great** leader. It takes intentionality on behalf of the potential leader to aid him/her

in their leadership quest.

ARE YOU READY?

_____

_____

_____

_____

_____

_____

_____

_____

_____

_____

_____

_____

ACTION

TIME FOR ACTION • TIME FOR ACTION •

ARE YOU READY?

_____

_____

_____

_____

_____

_____

_____

_____

_____

_____

ARE YOU READY?

_____

_____

_____

_____

_____

_____

_____

_____

_____

_____

_____

Chapter Six

People Focused versus Production Driven

One should not be so focused on the outcome that they forget about the people doing the work.

- Lisa Nanches Jackson

Great leaders are people focused rather than production driven. It is important to note that without people there can be no production. The challenge is for the leader or supervisor not to lose sight of this reality. Effective leaders must be able to work with people. Although in the workforce, people are paid to do a job it is important to understand that without people the job does not effectively get done. Characteristics of those who are **people-focused** are:

- they listen to their followers.

- they encourage their followers.

- they are empathic.

- they work to understand their

  followers.

- they appreciate their followers and the
  value they bring to the organization or
  team.

Production driven is when someone is

so focused on the ends that they lose sight of

the means. If the means justify the ends—you

should follow the rules no matter the

consequences. This means the actions people

take are justified regardless of how they go

about achieving their desired result. Follow

rules by telling the truth. Since the ends

justify the means - focus on the consequences

of an act instead of what you do. When the

means justify the ends, ethical consideration focuses on what you do, not the consequences of what you've done. Although the outcome, which is the work, must be accomplished, one should not be so focused on the outcome that they forget about the people doing the work. The leader has the responsibility to ensure that the job gets done and it is done correctly. The leader has a responsibility to ensure that people are producing. **Great** leaders can accomplish this while not losing sight that people are important.

Best Practices

❖ Take a step back when dealing with high-stress situations. Ensuring that the boundaries of mutual respect are maintained.

❖ Never compromise your integrity or work ethic to accomplish the job.

❖ Maintain professional boundaries but let your staff or team member know they matter.

❖ Be willing to listen or refer staff/team members to the proper resource(s) for assistance with problems.

❖ Exercise the Golden Rule, treat others the way you want to be treated. This term is often shared but seldom followed.

❖ Be willing to give people the benefit of the doubt.

Best Practices (Continued)

❖ Allow staff/team members to begin with a clean slate. In other words, do not hold past failures against them keeping in mind each new day presents an opportunity for change.

❖ Be willing to invest in the professional growth of staff/team members by offering training and upward mobility opportunities.

❖ When possible be willing to pitch-in and accept the ideas of staff/team members doing so helps them to feel they are contributing to the success of the mission.

❖ Make fairness and impartiality a priority. Showing favoritism can sabotage staff/team members' morale and negatively affect production.

ARE YOU READY?

_____

_____

_____

_____

_____

_____

_____

_____

_____

_____

_____

_____

ARE YOU READY?

_____

_____

_____

_____

_____

_____

_____

_____

_____

_____

ARE YOU READY?

_____

_____

_____

_____

_____

_____

_____

_____

_____

_____

_____

_____

Chapter Seven

Strategies for Transforming Toxic Work Environments

Great managers take control over their work environment, they do not allow the work environment to control them.

- Lisa Nanches Jackson

Great managers take control over their work environment, they do not allow the work environment to control them. They are agents of change and their presence makes the environment better.

A toxic workplace can be defined as a workplace where the people and/or atmosphere is unhealthy, and it affects one's personal life. **Five indicators of a Toxic Work Environment:**

1. Poor or lack of communication

2. Verbal abuse

3. The boss is self-centered

4. Low morale

5. High employee turnover

You can transform a toxic workplace! Begin by making a commitment that you will be a part of the solution and not the problem. Doing so will take effort because it takes less effort to point out what is wrong then it does to figure out what you can do to help make it right. I was in management\leadership for more than 25 years, so I know the weight and responsibility that one feels when they are a part of the "establishment," and the work environment is toxic. It is important that you realize you may not be able to do everything, but you can do some things to spark positive change. **Great** leaders become the catalyst for positive change.

One thing a toxic workplace can do is take your voice. When I say take your voice, I mean that it can silence or mute you. Being silenced or muted can make one feel helpless and hopeless. My advice for this situation is to refuse to be muted and reclaim your voice. This is achieved by taking advantage of the opportunities to offer positive solutions to workplace toxicity. Encourage people to take back their power and not allow their environment to dictate their disposition. Again, it may take more effort. It may not work the first time but stick to it. People will respect your stance.

Eight "R" Strategies for Transformation

1. Remain positive.

2. Refuse to surrender your voice.

3. Remember to leave work at work and don't allow it to affect your home life.

4. Respect and professionalism must be maintained although in instances it may not be warranted. We maintain our personal power when we do not allow people to dictate how we will act in various situations.

5. Rally others in the office to work toward positive change and having a

positive perspective toward the part that each person can play in eradicating a toxic environment.

6. Realize that self-care is important. Therefore, you need to take time to rest properly, relax and exercise.

7. Regular breaks are essential. Even if you bring your lunch, be intentional about stepping away during lunch, so that you can recharge and refocus.

8. Resolve that there are some challenges that are beyond your control, so you might need to seek another job.

ARE YOU READY?

_____

_____

_____

_____

_____

_____

_____

_____

_____

_____

_____

ARE YOU READY?

_____

_____

_____

_____

_____

_____

_____

_____

_____

_____

_____

_____

_____

ARE YOU READY?

_____

_____

_____

_____

_____

_____

_____

_____

_____

_____

_____

_____

_____

Chapter Eight

Managing in the Middle: The Successful Mid-Level Supervisor

A great leader can be effective
even in the middle.

- Lisa Nanches Jackson

Managing in the middle can be challenging, but a **great** leader can be effective even in the middle. The term managing in the middle speaks to the dynamics of a person that is a position where he/she can push things up for final decision, but not out for implementation. In this role the mid-level supervisor must be proficient in "Managing up." John Maxwell penned a book, the 360 Degree Leader: Developing Your Influence from Anywhere in the Organization. According to John C. Maxwell, "Ninety-nine percent of all leadership occurs not from the top but from the middle."[ii] One can lead up by doing your job with excellence, with a good attitude, with humility and show the value you add to the team, then you win the respect of the leader. Be determined to use your personal power instead of your positional power.

When one manages in the middle, he/she must be astute in determining when and how matters should be presented to upper management. One of the purposes of mid-level management is for the person to handle matters in his/her sphere of influence. Specifically, it is important to understand that not everything the staff wants needs to be presented. It has been my experience that it is better to hear, consider, and weigh the pros and cons of an idea in order to decide if it is one that should be presented to upper management. When considering a policy change, the mid-level manager should vet the idea to ensure the recommendation is fully explored, and they can intelligently answer questions that might be presented. This wisdom and expertise will be appreciated by upper management.

Mid-level managers must be courageous. They must be bold in order to be effective. A mid-level manager becomes the voice of those he/she leads. As such, the mid-level manager becomes an unofficial advocate. When the mid-level manager exhibits his/her good judgment and competence they will eventually earn the respect and in some instances the ear of upper management. Unfortunately earning the respect and the ear of upper management does not always yield the positive results that one would hope, which if one is not careful can lead to frustration. Therefore, it is important to anticipate frustration and come up with a method to handle it in a healthy manner. The success of being a mid-level manager can be found in following strategies:

- ❖ Maintain proper boundaries with your staff but let them know you are a part of the team.

- ❖ Exercise good judgment, so you know when a concern or an idea is ready to be presented to upper management.

- ❖ Be bold but use tact. It is important to be willing to speak up for your team, but it is equally important to be able to convey the message in such a way that it is heard.

- ❖ Set yourself up to be viewed as a problem-solver, not a person who causes problems. When presenting ideas or concerns ensure they are solution-focused and are tied to the organization's mission.

❖ Maintain your integrity and do not allow yourself to be used in the politics of the office.

❖ Lead in such a way that those you lead not only have a voice, but they have a vote. Specifically, be willing to hear out those on your team, when it makes sense to incorporate their ideas and allow them to have a say in matters that concern them.

Managing in the middle comes with many limitations, but it can also come with some advantages. The mid-level manager can speak truth to power. Use your voice to speak truth. Refuse to be a "yes man." People in leadership, whether they admit it or not need people that are willing to tell them truth. We all have blind spots. Many new vehicles now have indicators to let the driver know when there is a vehicle in the blind spot, so this minimizes collisions. Mid-level managers can be that indicator for upper management they can help avoid some unnecessary workplace collisions.

Great leaders make the most of their current position and never lose hope that one day they will reach the top. When you reach the top, remember what it was like to be in the middle and resolve to make the mid-level managers journey a little easier if you can. If this is done there can be a new and improved culture in the workplace where the Mid-level manager and upper management work as a team, which will make it better for the entire organization.

ARE YOU READY?

_____

_____

_____

_____

_____

_____

_____

_____

_____

_____

_____

_____

ACTION · TIME FOR ACTION ·

ARE YOU READY?

_____

_____

_____

_____

_____

_____

_____

_____

_____

_____

_____

_____

Chapter Nine

Walking the Fine Line Between Encouraging and Enabling

Great leaders are purposeful in identifying and developing the seed of greatness that lies within those they lead.

- Lisa Nanches Jackson

There is a fine line between encouraging and enabling a person. To many encouraging and enabling are similar terms, but when one enables it can have an adverse effect. The Oxford Dictionary defines the word encouraging as the act of giving somebody support, courage or hope. Another definition is to mentally support; to motivate, give courage, hope or spirit. Whereas the Oxford Dictionary defines word enabling as someone making it possible for something to happen or exist by creating the necessary conditions. **Great** leaders are encouragers and not enablers. They inspire with courage and confidence. They are purposeful in identifying and developing the seed of greatness that lies within those they lead. The difference between encouraging and enabling is when one encourages one provides mental or internal support. Conversely, when one enables a person, they provide external support. It is important to note that you cannot want something more for a person than they want for themselves. There must be a level of participation or work on behalf of the person if there is going to have sustainable success. There must be an investment by the employee or team member if there is to be true accomplishment. Enabling a person becomes a barrier to their success and true achievement. We enable people when we do for them what they can capably do for themselves, instead of providing them with the tools needed and supporting the doing.

A **great** leader realizes that followers, employees, and team players may have difficulty reaching his/her maximum potential. According to Ken Blanchard,[iii] "Recognition and Situational Leadership II" are four follower types. They are identified below, and each has its own characteristics. According to Blanchard, they are:

Low competence, High commitment;
Enthusiastic Beginner

This level is characterized by a low level of competence and yet, a high level of commitment. We all typically start here as new employees. The person is new and excited about getting to work but may not have all the skills to do the job.

Some competence, Low commitment;
Disillusioned Learner

The employee now has gained some competence or skills but his or her commitment takes a nosedive (low commitment), particularly if the job didn't add up to what he or she thought it would be.

The person has flashes of real competence,

he's sometimes overwhelmed and frustrated,

which has put a damper on his commitment.

High competence, variable commitment; Capable but Cautious Performer

This employee or follower type has a high

level of competence (they know the work),

but a variable commitment to the job. In other

words, they have good and bad days. The

employee has a good grasp of the job and is

working well, but he/she's hesitant to be out

there completely on his\her own. They may

become self-critical or even reluctant to trust his\her own instincts.

High competence, High commitment; Self-Reliant Achiever

These employees or followers are our star performers; they have a high level of both competence and commitment. They are ready to take on new challenges, work independently and often are the first ones to be promoted. They are justifiably confident because of his/her success and are able to work independently helping to inspire others.

Depending on the follower or employee, **great** leaders adjust their leadership style. However, the adjustment does not equal enabling. For instance, if you have an employee that is having a difficult time using computer software, you should provide the necessary training and coaching to use it. The employee still says that he/she is not comfortable using it and as a result you don't require the employee to use the software or you have someone else complete the task. This is called enabling. It is enabling because the employee is not being challenged to learn and operate the new software. They are being allowed to continue to use the excuse of incompetence. With the same scenario, encouraging would be providing the training and a software mentor. Allowing the person to use the software periodically until they become more proficient and challenging them to work outside of their comfort zone.

A skilled leader is one that can navigate situational leadership. A skilled leader can recognize the follower type they are encountering. An employee that is an *"Enthusiastic Beginner,"* will be willing to do what it takes to succeed, but they will not have the necessary skillset. The leader can encourage them by providing them with training, so they are enthusiastic and competent. The person then becomes a **Self-Reliant Achiever**. Whereas a **Disillusioned Learner** is an employee that has had the training, but he/she lacks the necessary commitment and motivation to do his/her job in the face of challenges. The skilled leader must be careful not to enable this person, because doing so could derail the person's road to acceptable performance. The Capable but Cautious Performer is an employee that is competent, but they lack confidence. Encouraging this person by providing regular feedback and allowing them to help with training new people one-on-one will go a long way to increasing their confidence.

ARE YOU READY?

_____

_____

_____

_____

_____

_____

_____

_____

_____

_____

_____

_____

ARE YOU READY?

_____

_____

_____

_____

_____

_____

_____

_____

_____

_____

_____

Chapter Ten

Do's and Don'ts of Leading

Don't be content with just watching what is happening, take the lead and make things happen.

- Lisa Nanches Jackson

Do Self-Manage. As a leader, you need to be able to manage your emotions, manage your time, manage your priorities, and manage your words. One cannot effectively manage others if they cannot manage themselves.

Don't Abuse Your Power. Maintaining appropriate professional boundaries is essential. It is unethical to require your staff to run your personal errands. The supervisor and employee relationship by nature is one of subordination. As such it is not really a request when an employee is asked by a supervisor to pick-up their clothes from the cleaners, to go grocery shopping or any other personal errand. The employee does not feel they can decline, because it may affect their job. **Great** leaders realize this dilemma and they don't do it.

Do Make Time. **Great** leaders make time for self-improvement. Investing in a professional coach or coaching sessions will be beneficial to enhancing your leadership.

Don't Enable. When we enable people, it encourages them to continue down the same road rather than challenging them to do better. Enabling people discourages them from thinking and it encourages dependence upon the leader/supervisor.

Do Hold Everyone Accountable.

Accountability across the board will cause key players to reflect on their actions and motives. This exercise can take your organization to the next level because it prompts people to change and improve.

Don't Forget to Help Others. It is easy to get caught up in focusing on our needs and just doing the job. However, we must be intentional about helping others and developing successors. There must be a plan of succession and the leader must participate in the preparation.

Do Treat People Fair. Philosopher John Rawls proposes a veil of ignorance as a way of testing for fairness. It's essentially wearing a blindfold, where you don't know your position, but you agree to make the rules based upon what is fair or just. The veil of ignorance is the idea that when you set up the rules, you don't get to know beforehand where you'll fall inside them, which is going to force you to construct things in a way that is really balanced and fair. This concept goes hand-and-hand with the Golden Rule.

Don't be Pessimistic. Being pessimistic means tending to see the worst aspect of things or believe that the worst will happen. **Great** leaders are optimistic. They defy the odds and they move forward with determination to make things happen. They look for people to improve and to become better. When optimism is consistently exhibited by the leader/supervisor/manager, it can slowly but surely become the culture. Simply put, optimism is looking at the glass half full as opposed to half empty.

Do What is Right. Far too many times leaders/supervisors/managers get pulled into "what is politically correct." I challenge you to resist the pull and to do what is right. Doing what is right is not always popular with the majority, but it is necessary if we hope to regain a standard of right and wrong.

Don't Relinquish Critical Decision-Making Power. The leader is ultimately responsible. Therefore, the leader owes it to the followers to allow critical matters to receive the consideration and determination and not his/her proxy.

Do Consider Other Perspectives.

Great leaders are open-minded and willing to

look at situations from various perspectives. When I conduct training sessions, I often do an exercise to show that sometimes things are neither right nor wrong but a matter of perspectives. Consider this example: '*YOUARENOWHERE*'. Some see You Are Now Here while others see You Are Nowhere. Both answers are correct. There are various reasons why people have different perspectives, some of the most common are sex, gender, and background. If we are going to effectively navigate through a diverse workplace or team, we must be willing to consider other perspectives.

Don't Forget to LEAD. You are the leader/supervisor so take charge, make good decisions, and be unyielding in your efforts to make your workplace or team better. Resolve to be a life-long learner, to encourage those you lead to be better than they ever imagined that they can be, be authentic so people will know you can be trusted to lead, and finally be determined to leave the position better than it was before you occupied it while taking the responsibility to prepare a competent successor.

ARE YOU READY?

_____

_____

_____

_____

_____

_____

_____

_____

_____

_____

_____

ARE YOU READY?

_____

_____

_____

_____

_____

_____

_____

_____

_____

_____

_____

_____

ARE YOU READY?

_____

_____

_____

_____

_____

_____

_____

_____

_____

_____

_____

_____

ARE YOU READY?

_____

_____

_____

_____

_____

_____

_____

_____

_____

_____

_____

_____

Endnotes

[i] Losada, Marxial and Emily Heaphy. American Behavioral Science. Volume: 47 issue: 6, page(s): 740-765. Issue published: February 1, 2004.

[ii] Maxwell, John C. The 360 Degree Leader: Developing Your Influence from Anywhere in the Organization. 2001, Thomas Nelson, Nashville, TN.

[iii] Blanchard, Kenneth. "Recognition and situational leadership II." *Emergency Librarian*, vol. 24, no. 4, 1997, p. 38. *Gale Academic Onefile*, Accessed 29 Oct. 2019.